CAREERS INSIDE THE WORLD OF

The Trades

You can learn about a trade in your school.

CAREERS & OPPORTUNITIES

CAREERS INSIDE THE WORLD OF
The Trades

by Peggy Santamaria

THE ROSEN PUBLISHING GROUP, INC.
NEW YORK

Published in 1995 by The Rosen Publishing Group, Inc.
29 East 21st Street, New York, NY 10010

First Edition

Manufactured in the United States of America

Library of Congress Cataloging-in-Publication Data

Santamaria, Peggy.
    Careers inside the world of trades / by Peggy Santamaria.—1st ed.
       p.   cm.—(Careers & opportunities)
    Includes bibliographical references and index.
    ISBN 0-8239-1898-X
1. Vocational guidance. 2. Skilled labor. 3. Artisans.
I. Title. II. Series.
HF5381.S277   1995
331.7'94 — dc20   95-19037
                                            CIP

Contents

TM

There are many training programs for work in the trades.

CHAPTER 1

CONSIDERING A CAREER IN THE TRADES: AN OVERVIEW

It's not a job, it's a career. That phrase may be familiar to you. But what does it mean? What is the difference between a job and a career? Both words refer to work, but dictionaries give different definitions. The word *job* may be defined as "task" or "routine"—not very exciting. For the word *career*, you are more likely to find a definition that refers to "one's life work" and "continuing growth in occupation."

Unlike a job, a career offers the opportunity to learn, to advance, to grow, and to earn more money. Given the choice, most people would prefer to have a career.

If you want a career but don't know where to find ideas of what you might do, start your search by simply looking around you. Yes, look at your home, your community. Everywhere you will see the products and the results of the work of

Women have careers in the trades.

women and men who have careers in the trades.

What are the trades? The term refers to a large group of skilled occupations including electrician, plumber, carpenter, stonemason, heavy equipment operator, and mechanic.

The people employed in the trades are very special. They have knowledge and skills acquired through training and hard work. They are recognized by society as having qualifications to perform work that others cannot do. They are specialists.

The trades workers know how to build homes and office buildings. They know how to repair engines and automobiles. They can weld steel and build bridges. They install and repair the electrical service that gives us light, heat, and television. They bring water into our homes as well as phone service. They help build rockets that travel into space and the roads we travel on each day. Men and women in the trades provide services that give us a better quality of life.

The training to learn the skills of a trade can take many forms. Classroom training and study are part of this process. High school classes, community college courses, technical schools, and trade union programs offer the necessary training.

Trade unions are organizations of workers that protect the interests of the workers in such matters as wages, working conditions, and hours. Trade unions provide financial assistance to members during sickness, strikes, unemployment, and old age. The unions also sponsor apprenticeship programs.

Another type of training is called "on-the-job training." The trainee works alongside a skilled worker, assisting, watching, listening, and learning. Many trade workers learned their specialized skills in this way.

A combination of the two types of training, that is, study and hands-on work, is probably the best preparation for a career.

Each trade career has steps of growth. In the

first step, apprenticeship, the apprentice works, learns low-level skills, and receives a lower rate of pay than the skilled trade worker. The duration of an apprenticeship depends on the requirements of the trade and the apprentice's speed of learning.

Each following step depends on the worker's desire to get ahead and willingness to continue learning.

The trades offer a wide variety of occupations. A hobby or interest of yours might transfer easily to a career in a trade. Opportunities in the trades, once limited to men, are now available to women on an equal basis.

If you think you might be interested in a trade career, find out if you are suited to it. School counselors, people already in the trades, and state and community agencies can provide information.

Questions to Ask Yourself

If you think you might want to have a career in a trade, first you should consider exactly what that would involve. 1) What is the difference between a job and a career? 2) What kinds of careers does the term "trade" include? 3) How can you learn a trade? 4) Why do you want to work in a trade?

CHAPTER 2

CAREERS IN CARPENTRY AND CONSTRUCTION

Janeen is a carpenter employed by a contractor who builds homes. She works from blueprints, using hand and power tools to cut, join, and install wood.

When Janeen was in high school she took a course in woodworking. She found she really enjoyed forming raw materials into something useful. Seeing a product result from her work was very satisfying.

Accuracy of measurement, Janeen found, was essential. She learned the meaning of the saying, "Measure twice, cut once." She learned to measure to 1/16 or 1/32 of an inch to make pieces of wood fit together exactly. This took patience and good eyesight.

Though Janeen had never enjoyed math in school, she found herself relying on it for all her work. The arithmetic she had struggled through began to make sense to her.

In woodshop Janeen also learned to handle tools. Being patient and precise helped her master the use of hammer and nails as well as power saws.

Janeen was particularly proud of a table she made in shop, and she gave it to her mother for Christmas. Her mother was very much impressed with the careful work Janeen had put into its construction. She suggested that Janeen consider carpentry as a trade. At first the idea surprised Janeen, but she was excited by the thought.

Carpentry became a serious consideration for Janeen. She decided to learn more about the trade. Her first step was to get a part-time job at a lumber and building-supply company. She enjoyed the job because she was not only earning money but also learning about tools, lumber, and the building industry.

At school Janeen signed up for a course in mechanical drawing to learn about drafting. She also continued to take wood shop.

On the job Janeen met building contractors. She finally got up the courage to ask one of them for a summer job, and she was hired. Her job was to assist the carpenters and do some heavy and dirty work, but she did not mind.

Janeen saw the carpenters build the framework of a house, put up the roof beams, build partitions for walls, install doors, put wood trim in

Carpentry can be very rewarding work.

This journeywoman carpenter is installing hardware on a door before hanging it.

place, and install cabinets. The work was hard. She was on her feet all day carrying materials, and she went home at night tired and in need of a shower. The summer passed quickly for Janeen, and soon it was time to go back to school.

The following summer Janeen returned to work for the contractor. This time she was allowed to do some simple carpentry work. Under the supervision of a skilled carpenter, she cut lumber and hammered nails. She worked very hard. Janeen believed that she had found work she could do well and be proud of. She could drive by a completed house and know that she had helped to build it. That was much more exciting than the job she once had selling hamburgers.

When Janeen graduated from high school, the building contractor hired her full time. Her career in carpentry had begun.

For five years Janeen has been pursuing her career. She attends home builders' seminars and keeps up with advances in building materials and methods. Her precision and dedication have benefited her. Recently her employer told her that before long she may advance to the position of supervisor.

Salaries for carpentry vary, depending on the type of work done and the geographical location. In the early 1990s the average wage for a carpenter was $412 per week. Some carpenters earned over $700 per week. Carpenters may work for building contractors or be self-employed. They may work in construction or in maintenance work.

Most carpenters learn their trade on the job. But apprenticeship programs are available through organizations like the National Association of Home Builders and the Associated Builders and Contractors.

Other trades in construction might interest you. If you don't think carpentry is your trade, look over some of the following for ideas.

Drywall Workers

Most walls and ceilings in houses, apartments, and commercial buildings are made from thin layers of gypsum between two layers of heavy paper. This material is called drywall or Sheetrock. Drywall workers measure, cut, and install the material over the wooden framework of the walls and ceiling. This is heavy, cumbersome work that requires a good eye and a steady hand.

Painters and Paperhangers

The tradespeople who apply paint and wallpaper to surfaces must know how each finish is applied and how to use the proper applicator. The surface must be cleaned, sanded, and properly prepared. The paint, varnish, stain, or paper must be skillfully applied for a smooth and even finish.

Carpet installers measure, cut, and install a carpet pad, then the carpet.

Insulation Workers

Insulation workers install various forms of insulation in homes and commercial buildings to reduce energy consumption. Insulation may be in rolls, sheets, or a form that is sprayed into place.

Carpet Installers

Nearly all new buildings are carpeted. The carpet installers measure, cut, and install first a carpet pad and then the carpeting. They use glues and nails. They also use a tool called a carpet kicker to stretch the carpet for a tight fit. Carpet installers often do their work on knee pads.

Roofers

Through on-the-job training or apprenticeship, the roofer learns to install and repair both flat roofs and slanted roofs. The work is often strenuous and sometimes dangerous. The roofer must apply insulation, then layers of waterproofing material, and finally the top layer of a glaze, gravel, or shingle material. Roofers may work for building contractors or be self-employed.

Questions to Ask Yourself

Carpentry and construction work can be difficult, but it is often rewarding. 1) What are some careers in the trades of carpentry and construction? 2) What skills do you think are necessary to be successful in carpentry or construction? 3) How can you acquire those skills?

CHAPTER 3

CAREERS IN THE ELECTRICAL TRADES

When Derrick was in high school he began to wonder what kind of job he would get after he graduated. He knew that many people were having trouble finding employment. His mother talked about people being laid off in the plant where she worked. Derrick wanted to be able to get a job that would be secure and pay well, but he had no idea what kind of work he could get. The only jobs he had had were delivering newspapers and working in a convenience store.

One day in the library Derrick saw a book about careers in electrical work. He checked the book out and took it home to read.

As Derrick walked home he thought about electricity. Electricity is everywhere, he thought—lights, TV, CD players, computers, microwaves. With so much power around, surely there must be lots of jobs working with electricity.

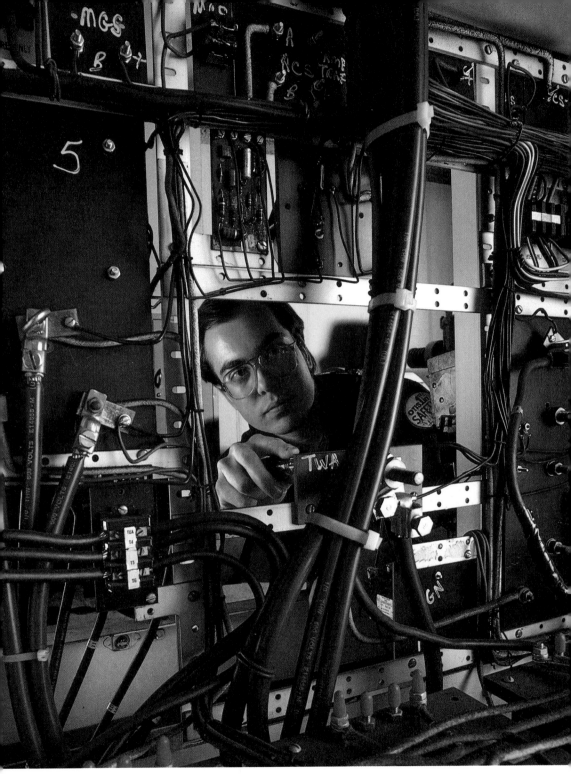

This service electrician is repairing an elevator control panel.

Reading the book, Derrick learned that electricians can work in either construction or maintenance and repair. In construction they work with blueprints to install electrical systems. They must follow the national and local electrical codes. First wires are brought into a building and placed in a wall or behind a panel. They are then pulled to outlets and fixtures. Circuit breakers, transformers, and other components may be used. Electricians often install the cable used for computers and phone systems. Good eyesight is a requirement for any electrician, because many wires are identified by color.

Electricians do a variety of maintenance work. Derrick learned that some work in factories where they maintain equipment, motors, and industrial robots. Others do only residential work, installing new wiring.

Derrick also learned that electricians may work with complex electronics. When doing this, they may work with another technician or an engineer.

Derrick read about the great range of salaries electricians earn, depending on where they live. The average salary in 1990 was $524 per week.

Jobs for electricians are expected to increase over the next ten to fifteen years. Layoffs are fewer than in other construction trades.

Derrick was very much interested in what he

read. An electrical trade sounded like a career with a good future, a good income, and steady employment. He decided to talk about it to the guidance counselor at school.

Ms. Johnston, the guidance counselor, gave Derrick information about apprenticeship programs for electricians. In such programs, usually four to five years long, the apprentice attends classes for about 144 hours each year. On-the-job training totals 8,000 hours. The apprentice learns blueprint reading, math, electrical theory, electronics, electrical codes, and safety. He or she also learns to drill holes, set up conduits, install and test wires, and diagram electrical layouts. Apprenticeship pay is between 38 percent and 50 percent of the experienced electricians' pay; it increases with experience and skill.

When he graduated from high school, Derrick applied for an apprenticeship and was accepted. He began his training in the classroom and on-the-job. He received pay as he learned.

After completing the apprenticeship program, Derrick had to be licensed by the state in which he lives. This required a test, but Derrick was well prepared for it.

Not all electricians are trained through formal apprenticeships. Some begin as helpers and learn by working with a licensed electrician.

Other kinds of work are similar to or related to

the electrician's work. The following are a few examples.

Line Installers, Splicers, and Repairers

The lines move electricity from the powerplant to the home or business. They bring phone service and TV cable as well. The installer may bury the cable and wires or set up poles and work high above the ground. The splicer connects these wires so that the circuit is complete. The repairer fixes damaged wires.

Electronic Equipment Repairers

These skilled workers repair and maintain many kinds of equipment in homes, businesses, hospitals, and aircraft. They work on telephone systems, computers, radar, and medical diagnostic equipment. Formal training is available in community colleges and technical schools. On-the-job training may also qualify for entry-level employment.

Elevator Installers and Repairers

The men and women of this trade construct, install, repair, and maintain elevators and escalators. They work from blueprints and must have a knowledge of electricity and electronics. They install cables and wires and must lift and carry heavy equipment. Formal training is necessary for this work.

Appliance repair people may have to go to someone's home to fix a large appliance.

Home Appliance and Power Tool Repairers

These trade workers are trained to diagnose and repair many electrical systems. Among them are ovens, washers, dryers, vacuum cleaners, and power tools. Classroom training as well as on-the-job training are preparation for this career.

Questions to Ask Yourself

Electrical work is a very interesting and stable career. In today's world, electricity is all-important; so is the person who keeps it on. 1) What does an electrician do? 2) Where can an electrician work? 3) What are other kinds of careers within the electrical trade?

CHAPTER 4

CAREERS IN METALWORKING

Greg is a metalworker. He is a welder. Greg uses a gas torch to cut metal. He welds pieces of metal together to form a strong, lasting bond. He works wearing a protective hood and face shield and heavy gloves.

When Greg was little he frequently visited his grandfather's welding shop. His grandfather did jobs for farmers in the area, making frames for hay wagons and repairing farm equipment.

When Greg was twelve years old, his grandfather began teaching him about welding equipment. Greg learned how pieces of metal could be fused or joined together by using just the right amount of heat from the welding rod. It takes time and patience to learn to adjust the temperature for a strong weld.

In high school Greg took metal shop. He became so good in his class that his teacher

It takes a lot of training to become a good welder.

would invite him to other classes to show students and teachers how to do certain welds.

In the afternoons Greg worked with his grandfather, learning and practicing his skills.

Greg learned to read blueprints and instructions for the job to be done. He learned to use grinders and chipping hammers to remove rough edges from welded surfaces.

Welding required Greg to learn patience. He needed steady hands and eyes to concentrate on the piece of metal he was welding. He found that working with such attention to detail and with slow steady movements could be as tiring as lifting heavy boxes all day.

Working with open flame is dangerous. Greg needed protective clothing. Flashes from the welding torch can injure eyes, so he always wore his hood and face shield.

After high school graduation Greg was hired by a construction company as a welder. Working high above the ground, he bolted and welded the steel beams that form the inner structure of large buildings. Greg enjoyed seeing a project develop and become real. He liked to read the blueprint, prepare the materials, connect them, and then see a finished product. A welder, he says, needs to be able to see the big picture and know how it is supposed to turn out.

Having worked as a welder for a few years, Greg felt ready to take the tests for certification.

States offer certificates in different welding techniques: vertical, horizontal, on flat surfaces, and overhead. Once certified in these techniques, a welder can be considered for the more difficult, demanding, and high-paid jobs.

Greg became an accomplished, successful welder. Through his employer, he had opportunities to attend seminars given by manufacturers of welding materials, enabling him to keep to up-to-date with new technology.

Whether you live in a rural area, a large city, or a small town, welding jobs are probably available near you. Welders construct and repair ships, cars, and even spacecraft. They manufacture thousands of products used in business and industry. Some welding businesses are huge and employ many workers; some are small shops with a few workers; some are individuals who handle local jobs from a small garage.

A career in welding offers many opportunities to hard-working, qualified men and women. Though the work is demanding and tiring, it does not always require great physical strength. Steady eyes and steady hands, however, are absolutely necessary. Blueprint reading, math skills, and mechanical drawing are helpful in welding.

Salaries earned by welders are based on the level of skill required and the type of industry. In the early 1990s salaries for welders across the

Welders must wear protective equipment.

Machinists must pay attention to every detail.

country ranged from $24,900 to $44,900 per year.

Besides welding, other jobs are available for those who enjoy working with metal.

Machinists

Machinists produce small, precise metal parts used to build or repair machinery, cars, airplanes, and many other things. The machinist works from blueprints to create the parts and often uses high-speed machinery. Generally a formal apprenticeship is required to become a machinist.

Tool and Die Makers

Tools and dies are parts of machines that make metal products. Tools are parts that hold the metal in place; dies are used to shape and form the metal. Tool and die makers operate precision machinery and must know math and blueprint reading. They are paid well for the skills that they learn in vocational schools and through apprenticeship.

Sheetmetal Workers

Many necessary items are made of thin sheets of metal. Heating and air-conditioning systems, roofs, siding, restaurant equipment, and duct work are only a few of them. Sheetmetal work may be done in a shop or on the job site.

Numerical-Control Machine Tool Operators

These operators may work with metal or plastic. They cut and form the material to make parts for machines and many products. They work with machines that are computer-programmed for the sizes and shapes they need.

Jewelers

A different type of metal worker is a jeweler. Jewelers repair, adjust, and make jewelry from metals and gemstones. The work requires steady hands, steady eyes, patience, and attention to detail. It does not require physical strength. Most jewelers are employed in department stores or jewelry shops.

Questions to Ask Yourself

Metalworking is more of an art than a trade. It can be tiring and dangerous, but can also be beautiful. 1) What does a metalworker do? 2) What skills does metalworking require? 3) What are other kinds of careers within the metalworking trade?

CHAPTER 5

CAREERS IN AUTOMOTIVE TRADES

Jason has been interested in cars for as long as he can remember. When his dad tuned up the car or changed the spark plugs, Jason was right beside him trying to see what was going on under the hood. He asked a lot of questions.

In high school, Jason signed up for a course in automobile mechanics. The instructor gave the students the chance to work on engines, do tune-ups, and learn to make minor repairs. The more Jason learned, the more interested he became.

At sixteen, Jason got a part-time job in a gasoline service station, filling gas tanks, cleaning windshields, and checking oil levels. Whenever possible he watched the mechanics at work and asked questions. He saw them lifting heavy parts, working in cramped positions, and sometimes getting cut or burned. They got very dirty and greasy and smelled of oil and gasoline.

Classroom training as well as hands-on training are sometimes required for a mechanic.

One day Jason told the station owner that he thought he might drop out of school and work full time at the station. Mr. Graham said that was not a good idea. He told Jason that to be a good automobile mechanic he needed not only to finish school but take even more courses. He said that many skills were required of a good mechanic. Reading is important because the manuals that mechanics use are very technical and difficult. As cars become more complex, so does the mechanic's job.

34   Jason also learned from Mr. Graham that

to get a good job and advance in the trade, a mechanic should be certified. Certification is awarded by the NIASE, the National Institute for Automotive Service Excellence. It requires that mechanics have two years of experience and then pass a test. Mr. Graham explained that there are several areas of certification such as engine repair, brake repair, and electrical systems. Once certified, a mechanic must be tested again every five years.

Jason took Mr. Graham's advice. He stayed in high school and graduated. Then he attended a community college and earned an Associate degree in automobile mechanics. This school was certified by NATEF, the National Automotive Technicians Education Foundation, which rates schools on education and equipment.

Jason became a full-time mechanic at Mr. Graham's service station. After one year of work he was able to qualify for his ASE certification test in engine repair. Because of his degree in automobile mechanics, he did not need the usual two years of experience before taking the test.

Jason's workdays are very busy. He diagnoses problems in engines, sometimes test-driving the car to see what seems to be wrong. He then uses a variety of electronic diagnostic machines to help him pinpoint the problem. He also works with hand tools and power tools.

Jason is doing something he has always

enjoyed. He plans to become certified in all the areas of automotive mechanic work. Someday he would like to have his own service station.

The career Jason has chosen in the automotive trades is one that will offer him many opportunities. Besides working at the service station, he could get a job with a car dealership, an independent repair shop, or start his own repair business.

Highly skilled automobile mechanics earned an average of over $18 per hour in the early 1990s. Those with less skill earned an average of $9 per hour.

Other careers are open in the automotive field. Let's look at some of the options.

Auto Painter

Auto painters remove the old paint from cars and prepare the surface for applying new paint. This may include repairing nicks in surfaces. The auto painter works with toxic fumes and must wear a respirator and mask. The work is mentally tiring and requires attention to detail. Apprenticeship or on-the-job training is required.

Auto Body Repairer

Auto body repairers fix parts of car bodies that have been damaged in accidents. They may use metal or plastic to reshape the auto. The work can be dirty and strenuous. Courses in automobile repair and mechanics in high school can help you get an apprenticeship or on-the-job training for this career.

Automotive Repair Service Estimator

The estimator studies a damaged vehicle and estimates the cost and time required to repair it. The estimator needs to have technical knowledge of all auto repairs and costs of parts and labor as well as good communication skills.

Diesel Mechanic

Diesel engines are found in buses, ships, cars, trucks, railroad trains, generators, and construction and farm machines. The diesel mechanic is able to take apart a diesel engine, check for malfunction, and make the necessary repairs. The work can be strenuous. Good reading ability as well as courses in science and math are helpful. Vocational courses are available.

Motorcycle Mechanic

Motorcycle mechanics service, adjust, repair, and lubricate motorcycle engines. They generally specialize in one type of motorcycle, because most are employed by dealers. Formal training in motorcycle mechanics increases the opportunity for employment, and high school courses in automobile mechanics are helpful.

Questions to Ask Yourself

If you've always loved cars, a career in the automotive trades might be for you. It requires skill, patience and dedication. 1) What kinds of courses help enhance skills for a career in the automotive trades? 2) Where can you work as an automotive mechanic? 3) What other careers are open in the automotive field?

CHAPTER 6

CAREERS IN TRANSPORTATION

When Kathy graduated from high school, she wasn't sure what she wanted to do. She went to work in the office of a bank. She was very responsible and efficient, needing little or no supervision. But despite her success, Kathy felt that there was something she would rather be doing. Soon she realized that she wanted to be out on the road, not at a desk.

The idea of being a truck driver was very appealing. But Kathy had a baby daughter. As a truck driver she would need to be away from home for long hours and in some cases for days. She did not want to do that.

Kathy went to the local school board for information about driving a school bus. There she learned that she would need a commercial drivers license (CDL). The school board offered classes on bus driving.

School bus drivers have to love working with kids.

Kathy began studying, going to classes, and learning about buses. She had to learn all about gas engines, diesel engines, air brakes, fluid systems, exhaust systems, hoses, and belts. She had to learn how to handle a large bus on a busy street and on a highway. She also had to learn how to maneuver a large, heavy vehicle safely in snow and on icy roads. The work was very hard, and it took many weeks, but Kathy stuck with it.

While learning to master the huge bus, Kathy was also learning about state and federal highway regulations.

When Kathy passed her final tests, she got her CDL and was qualified by the school board to handle a school bus. Next she had to pass a physical examination and an eye test.

When there was a vacancy, Kathy was hired as a school bus driver. Her training continued in required sessions to learn how to interact with the children, how to handle problems among them, how to administer CPR and first aid, and what to do in the event of an accident.

Kathy's job is a very responsible position. Each morning before starting her route she needs to examine the bus, checking the engine, the belts, and the hoses, the wheels, the exhaust system, and the lights.

Kathy is pleasant and friendly with the young people on her bus. However, she must also be firm. Safety may require that she be strict at times. As a driver, Kathy must be aware of what is going on among the children and on the road behind her, in front of her, and on either side of her. Every year she must have a physical examination and a driving test.

Kathy's work offers her a sense of independence and responsibility. Her schedule allows her time with her young daughter and time to take courses at the community college. Some day, when her daughter is grown, Kathy may pursue the career of a truck driver.

If you want to learn more about opportunities as a school bus driver, speak to your school officials. Job openings for school bus drivers are expected to increase through 2005. In the early 1990s the average school bus driver's salary was over $9.50 per hour.

There are many other career opportunities for those who want to operate large vehicles. The following are but a few.

Commercial Bus Driver

A commercial bus driver may operate a city bus, an intercity bus, or a cross-country bus. All must have a CDL, be in good physical condition, and have good vision and a good driving record.

Truck Driver

Truckers may deliver goods from one state to another or simply across town. Most truck drivers are required to have a CDL. Interstate truck drivers are subject to federal as well as state regulations. High school classes in automobile mechanics and driver's education can be helpful in obtaining truck-driving jobs. Some vocational schools also offering training in truck driving.

Material Moving Equipment Operator

Material moving equipment operators also sit behind the wheel of a large powerful vehicle, but they do not transport people or goods; they transport materials. These drivers operate bulldozers, cranes, and graders. They work at construction sites and on bridges and highways. Most of the training for a material moving equipment operator is obtained on-the-job. Apprenticeship programs are available for training on a wider range of equipment.

Questions to Ask Yourself

A career in the transportation field can be appealing if you like to travel and don't want to sit in an office all the time. It requires a lot of time, but can allow you to see many new places. 1) What are some careers available within the field of transportation? 2) What are the benefits and drawbacks to having a career in transportation?

CHAPTER 7

CAREERS IN PLUMBING AND RELATED TRADES

Eight years ago Mark was working for a building contractor as a construction laborer. He worked at the site helping the carpenters and drywall workers by carrying materials and tools and keeping the work area clear.

Joe Davis was a plumber working at the same job site. Impressed by Mark's serious attitude and efficiency, he asked if Mark would like to earn extra money by helping him install the plumbing in a house he was building for his family. Mark was eager to do so.

Mark watched Mr. Davis as he measured, cut, and installed pipe. He tried to help and learn as much as he could. When the plumbing work on the house was done, Mr. Davis offered Mark a job as a plumber's assistant with his company. He said Mark would be able to learn the trade by working with him and the other skilled plumbers.

Work in plumbing requires a lot of other skills such as welding.

Mark took the job, and his apprenticeship in plumbing began.

The most important job of the plumber, Mark learned, is to bring clean water into a building and remove all waste water from the building. To accomplish this, the plumber digs ditches and lays pipe from the main water supply to the building. The plumber works with blueprints to see where the pipes will run to supply bathrooms, kitchens, heating areas, and drinking fountains.

The pipe, made of copper or plastic, must be cut to the proper lengths and angles before it can be installed. Mark was glad he had taken geometry **45** in high school; it helped him understand how to measure angles.

Mark learned how to cut the pipe using special cutting tools. The pieces of pipe then had to be fastened together. Metal pipe is welded; plastic pipe is cemented.

While installing pipe in a building, the plumber may work in the same area as other tradespeople. Carpenters, plumbers, electricians, and others must schedule their work.

The plumber's work includes installing such fixtures as bathtubs, showers, toilets, sinks, dish-washers, and washing machines.

Mark found that he often had to work under difficult conditions. Frequently he had to be out-side in bad weather. Other times he worked in cramped areas like crawl spaces.

Mark also learned about regulations. Each locality has building and plumbing codes that specify what size pipe and what kinds of materials can be utilized.

After working as an apprentice plumber for Mr. Davis for four years, Mark was eligible to take the test to become a journeyman, a plumber who is licensed to work in the trade. Mark began to study for the written part of the test. In an apprenticeship program, he would have attended classes; however, there were no openings in the program in his area.

Mark passed his test and became a licensed

plumber. Now he could work more independently and earn more money.

Mark continued to study and to attend builders' seminars to keep up with advances in the building and plumbing industries. He also took extra courses at a community college.

After two years as a journeyman, Mark decided to qualify as a master plumber, the highest level a licensed plumber can reach. When he applied to take the test, Mark was given a reading list of books to study. He also enrolled in a course at the community college. Mark had to work very hard, doing his job during the day, and studying and going to classes at night.

When Mark finally took the test, he passed and became a master plumber. All his hard work had paid off. Today Mark is a plumbing inspector for his county, earning a good salary. He is responsible for checking the installation of plumbing in residential and commercial buildings in the county. He must be sure that code requirements are followed and that all plumbing is safe and effective.

Plumbing offers many opportunities in both construction and maintenance and repair. Apprenticeship earnings may only be 50 percent of the licensed plumber's rate. In the early 1990s the national average salary for plumbers was $508 per week.

If you think you may be interested in plumb-

Formal training is required to be a pipefitter.

ing, here are some related careers you might consider.

Pipefitter
A pipefitter installs and repairs pipe systems used to cool or heat buildings, for generating electricity, or in manufacturing. Formal vocational training and apprenticeship are needed for this career.

Steamfitter
The steamfitter also installs pipe systems. Usually working in an industrial setting, the steamfitter

follows blueprints and specifications to measure,

cut, and connect pipes to move gas and steam under high pressure.

Sprinklerfitter

Installing automatic fire protection sprinkler systems is the job of the sprinklerfitter. The fitter connects the sprinkler pipes to the water supply system. In many areas the building codes require that all new commercial and public buildings have sprinklers. Many city governments are requiring that existing buildings be upgraded. In some places sprinkler systems are being installed in residences. Formal training, apprenticeship, or on-the-job training are required for this career.

Heating and Air-Conditioning Technician

This technician works with wires, pipes, motors, and compressors and must be able to read and understand blueprints and specifications. Technical school training and apprenticeship are needed for this trade. Some on-the-job training is available.

Questions to Ask Yourself

There are many opportunities for careers out there for someone interested in plumbing. 1) What is the most important job of a plumber? 2) How can you become a plumber? 3) What are other careers related to the plumbing trade?

CHAPTER 8

GETTING THE JOB YOU WANT

If you have chosen a career, congratulations! If you are ready to do research through reading and talking to people, good luck to you in this phase of your career development.

As you make your plans and chart your course, there is a part of the success process that we have not yet talked about. Besides the technical skills you need, there are personal skills you will want to work on. When you have become proficient in your trade skills, you will need to be able to convince an employer that you are the person for the job.

Let's look at three skills that will help you get the position you want.

Writing Skills

To get the attention of an employer, you will

50 probably first send a letter and a résumé. A

résumé is a summary of the things you have learned and done that qualify you for a particular job. It should represent all your good qualities and accomplishments.

Many books are available that can help you learn to write letters and résumés. Your guidance counselor at school or an assistant at the library can help you get the information you need.

Speaking Skills

An interview with an employer gives you an opportunity to make a good impression. Speaking clearly and politely is very important. If the employer cannot hear you, he or she may never know that you are capable of doing a good job.

Information is available in books and on videos that can help you develop good interviewing techniques. Check with a teacher or a librarian for help in getting material on improving your speaking skills.

Grooming Skills

A neat, clean appearance is a must for a job interview. You may be applying for a job as an automobile mechanic. You know that the work will be dirty, but that does not mean it is acceptable to go to the interview with greasy hands and oil-stained clothing.

For an interview for any job, you should have

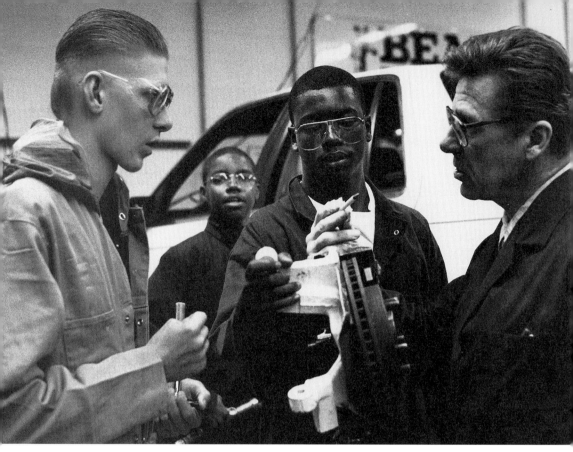
You must have both good personal skills and technical skills to get a job.

clean hair, clean hands, and clean face. Your clothing should also be neat and clean.

Check in your school or public library for books giving tips on good grooming. Learning to look your best will make you feel good about yourself not just when you are on an interview, but all the time.

Choosing your career path and making the commitment to the hard work that it will require is exciting. Remember that though there is much to be done, there is much you can accomplish.

Go for it!

Questions to Ask Yourself

There are many other skills that are just as important to getting a job as actual knowledge of the trade. Think about how you can develop these skills. 1) What is a résumé? 2) What are some questions that an interviewer might ask you? 3) Where can you find more information on tips for getting a job?

GLOSSARY

apprentice Person learning a job through training on the job and in a classroom.

building code Laws stating the types of materials and methods of construction to be used.

blueprint Drawing used in construction that is reproduced in blue lines.

CDL Commercial driver's license, required for people who operate large vehicles.

certification Official statement that someone is qualified to perform skilled work.

contractor Person or company who agrees to perform certain tasks stated in a contract.

drafting Drawing or designing the exact measurements to be used in construction.

journeyperson Someone who has completed an apprenticeship and is a skilled worker.

résumé Summary of one's employment, education, and accomplishments.

specifications Detailed descriptions of materials and measurements to be used in construction.

54 **technical school** School that specializes in

teaching skills needed for trades and other occupations. Also called *vocational school.*

trade union Organization of workers to protect
interests in wages, working conditions, and
benefits.

APPENDIX

The following organizations may be useful in following up an interest in a particular trade.

CARPENTRY

Associated Builders and Contractors
729 15th Street NW
Washington, DC 20005

International Brotherhood of Painters and Allied Trades
1750 New York Avenue NW
Washington, DC 20006

National Association of Home Builders, Home Builders Institute
15th & M Streets NW
Washington, DC 20005

National Insulation and Abatement Contractors Association
99 Canal Center Plaza
56 Alexandria, VA 22314

National Roofing Contractors Association
10255 West Higgins Road
Rosement, IL 60018

**United Union of Roofers, Waterproofers &
    Allied Workers**
1125 17th Street NW
Washington, DC 20036

ELECTRICAL TRADES

Appliance Service News
P.O. Box 789
Lombard, IL 60148

Communication Workers of America
1925 K Street NW
Washington, DC 20006

Electronics Technicians Association
604 North Jackson
Greencastle, IN 46135

Independent Electrical Contractors, Inc.
P.O. Box 10379
Alexandria, VA 22310

**International Brotherhood of Electrical
    Workers**
1125 15th Street NW
Washington, DC 20005

National Electrical Contractors
7315 Wisconson Avenue
Bethseda, MD 20814

METALWORKING

American Welding Society
550 LeJeune Road
Miami, FL 33135

International Association of Machinists
  Aerospace Workers
1300 Connecticut Avenue NW
Washington, DC 20036

Jewelers of America
1185 Avenue of the Americas
New York, NY 10036

National Tooling and Machining Association
9300 Livingstone Road
Fort Washington, MD 20744

Sheet Metal & Air Conditioning Contractors
  National Association
4201 Lafayette Center Drive
Chantilly, VA 22021

AUTOMOTIVE CAREERS

Automotive Service Association, Inc.
P.O. Box 929
Bedford, TX 76021-0929

Automotive Service Industry Association
444 North Michigan Avenue
Chicago, IL 60611

Chrysler Dealer Apprenticeship Program
National C.A.P. Coordinator
CIMS 423-21-06
26001 Lawrence Avenue
Center Line, MI 48015

Ford Motor Company
ASSET Program, Training Department
3000 Schaefer Road
Dearborn, MI 48121

General Motors Automotive Service Education Service Program
National College Coordinator
30501 Van Dyke Avenue
Warren, MI 48090

Motorcycle Mechanics Institute
2844 West Deer Valley Road
Phoenix, AZ 85027

National Association of Trade and Technical Schools
Dept. BL, P.O. Box 2006
Annapolis Junction, MD 20701-2006

National Automotive Technicians Education Foundation
13505 Dulles Technology Drive
Hearndon, VA 22071-3415

TRANSPORTATION CAREERS

American Bus Association
1015 15th Street NW
Washington, DC 20005

American Public Transit Association
1201 New York Avenue NW
Washington, DC 20005

American Trucking Associations, Inc.
2200 Mill Road
Alexandria, VA 22314

Industrial Truck Association
1750 K Street NW
Washington, DC 20006

International Union of Operating Engineers
1125 17th Street NW
Washington, DC 20036

National School Transportation Association
P.O. Box 2639
Springfield, VA 22152

Professional Truck Driver Institute of America
8788 Elk Grove Boulevard
Elk Grove, CA 95624

PLUMBING

Air Conditioning and Refrigeration Institute
1501 Wilson Boulevard
Arlington, VA 22209

Associated Builders and Contractors
729 15th Street NW
Washington, DC 20005

Mechanical Contractors Association of America
1385 Piccard Drive
Rockville, MD 20850

National Association of Plumbing, Heating and Cooling Contractors
P.O. Box 6808
Falls Church, VA 22040

National Fire Sprinkler Association
P.O. Box 1000
Patterson, NY 12563

FOR FURTHER READING

Bingham, Mindy, and Stryker, Sandy. *Career Choices: A Guide for Teens and Young Adults.* Santa Barbara, CA: Able Publishing, 1990.

Encyclopedia of Careers and Vocational Guidance. Chicago: J.G. Ferguson Publishing Co., 1990.

Exploring Careers. Indianapolis: JIST Works, Inc., 1990.

Lederer, Muriel. *Blue Collar Jobs for Women.* New York: E.P. Dutton, 1979.

Lytle, Elizabeth Stewart. *Careers in the Construction Trades.* New York: Rosen Publishing Group, 1992.

———. *Careers as an Electrician.* New York: Rosen Publishing Group, 1993.

Occupational Outlook Handbook. Washington, DC: Bureau of Labor Statistics, U.S. Department of Labor.

Schauer, Donald D. *Careers in Trucking.* New York: Rosen Publishing Group, 1991.

INDEX

63

ACKNOWLEDGMENTS
Special thanks to Garland Maust, Kathy Wiley, and Mark Santamaria for sharing their experiences and knowledge with me.

ABOUT THE AUTHOR
Peggy Santamaria works in community mental health. She develops and implements educational and advocacy programs. She and her husband have built their own home on a wooded mountainside in western Maryland. There they are able to enjoy hiking, photography, and gardening. They have three daughters.

COVER PHOTO: © Maria Taglienti/Image Bank
PHOTO CREDITS: Impact Visuals: pp. 2, 14 © Martha Tabor, p. 6 © H.L. Delgado, p. 8 © Dana Schuerholz, p. 48 © Harvey Finkle, pp. 34, 52 © Jim West; Image Bank: p. 13 © Larry Pierce, p. 17 William Rivelli, pp. 20, 24 © Walter Bibikow, p. 26 © A. Satterwhite, p. 29 © Steve Dunwell, p. 30 © Erik Leigh Simmons, p. 40 © David W. Hamilton, p. 45 © Francesco Ruggeri
PHOTO RESEARCH: Vera Ahmadzadeh
DESIGN: Kim Sonsky